The ELECTRICITY Mystery

Lisa Trumbauer

Contents

Rigby

A Harcourt Achieve Imprint

www.Rigby.com
1-800-531-5015

Introducing Professor Max Power!

Hello, young scientists! I'm Professor Maxwell Power. You can call me Professor Power, although I sometimes go by Max Power when I'm really charged up. Anything's fine as long as you don't call me "Pumpkin." That's what my Aunt Martha calls me when she pinches my cheeks.

You want to know what's cooking in my lab? Electricity! Electricity is my specialty. I've experimented with electricity, I've studied electricity, I've done tricks with electricity—I've even named my pet rock Electricity, though he never has learned to come when I call him.

Electricity is a very useful and important part of our daily lives, yet what electricity is and how it works can seem like a mystery. You can't see electricity, but you can definitely see what it can do. In fact, your life would be very different without it.

I've received a ton of e-mails from kids wanting to get the scoop on electricity. I've pulled a handful of them to tackle, so read on as I try to dig up some answers. Maybe together we can solve the electricity mystery!

Chapter 1

Max's Crash Course in Electricity

To: ProfMaxPower

From: BenJSmith

Professor Power, I've heard about electricity, but what exactly is it?

Well, Ben, what we call electricity can also be called *electric energy* because electricity is a form of energy. For centuries scientists knew that electricity existed, but they didn't quite understand what it was or where it came from. It wasn't until the 19th century that scientists had the tools to figure out what electric energy was.

Electricity is produced from the basic building blocks of everything on the planet—**atoms**. Atoms are super-small **particles** that join together to form **molecules**, and molecules join together to form **matter**. Atoms, particles, and molecules are so small, they are almost impossible to see, even with the most powerful microscopes.

While it makes for a good scary story, electricity does not make monsters.

What's the Matter?

Almost everything in the universe can be summed up in just one word—matter. Matter can be solid, liquid, or gas. When matter is solid, all the molecules inside it are bunched tightly together. When matter is liquid, the molecules flow, or move around. When matter is a gas, the atoms are spread far apart, and they move around a lot.

solid	liquid	gas
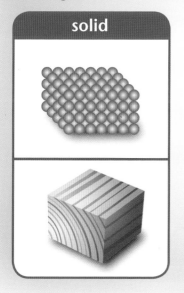	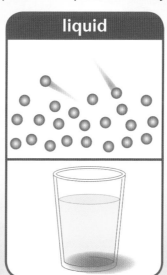	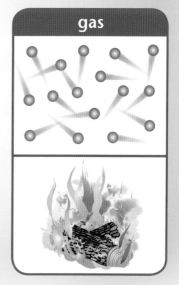

Parts of an Atom

Atoms are made up of very tiny particles. The center of the atom is called the nucleus, which is made of proton particles and neutron particles. Protons have a positive charge, and neutrons don't have any charge at all. Moving around outside the nucleus are electrons, which have a negative charge.

Not all atoms are the same. There are 106 different types of atoms with different numbers of particles inside them. The atom seen below is a sodium atom, and it has 11 electrons floating around it. Sodium atoms are used to make salt.

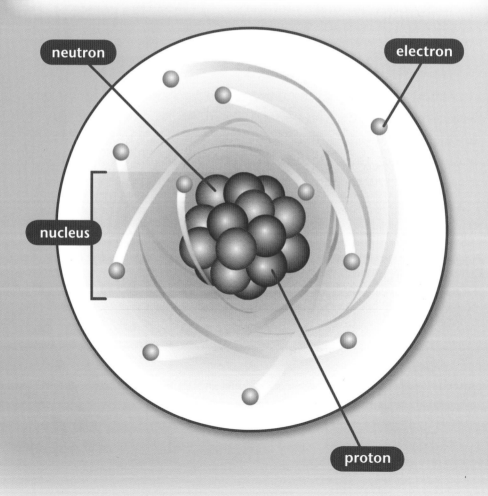

Electricity is Made

Sometimes atoms trade electrons back and forth. The electrons break free from one atom and jump over to the next. When this happens, it causes an electric charge. This charge moves between the two atoms. Break enough electrons off from their atoms, and you've got electricity! Do this with billions and billions of atoms, and you're on your way to powering the **appliances** in your home.

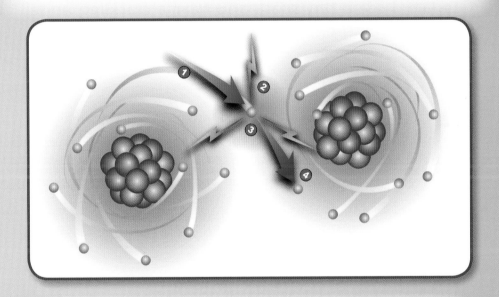

1 Electron breaks free of atom.

2 "Breaking" causes electric charge.

3 Electron jumps to new atom.

4 Electron becomes part of the new atom.

To: ProfMaxPower

From: DaisyFlower

Max Power, whenever I take socks out of the dryer, they're stuck together. When I pull them apart, I see a tiny spark and hear a crackling noise. What's going on?

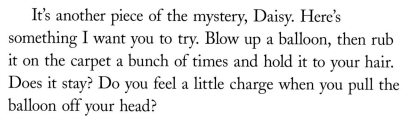

It's another piece of the mystery, Daisy. Here's something I want you to try. Blow up a balloon, then rub it on the carpet a bunch of times and hold it to your hair. Does it stay? Do you feel a little charge when you pull the balloon off your head?

Socks out of the dryer stick together for the same reason the balloon sticks to your hair—**static** electricity. Static electricity is electric energy that's sitting still. It's waiting to move. While in the dryer, the atoms that make up the sock pick up a lot of extra electrons from the other clothes and the dryer's hot air. But these electrons just sit there in the sock's atoms, building up a stronger and stronger charge.

When you put together two objects that have lots of atoms with lots of electrons and really strong charges, they stick together. As long as the objects don't move, you've got static electricity. But pull them apart, and the electrons really start jumping around! You get plenty of atom-hopping and a little jolt of electricity.

Static electricity can be a little hair-raising at times. Static electrons build up in this girl's ski cap, but when she takes it off, those electrons sure aren't static anymore!

To: ProfMaxPower

From: BMXRacer

Max, what would our lives be like without electricity?

They'd be a whole lot different, I can tell you that, Racer. With no electric lights, most of your daily activities would have to be done by the light of the sun. That means you'd have to punch a lot more windows in your house so you could let in as much sunlight as possible. At night you'd use candles, oil lamps, or torches to see, and those give off a lot of smoke and soot inside the house. Plus, you'd have a lot of chimneys to sweep.

However, you would be thankful for all those extra windows and fires, because there'd be no electric heating or air conditioning during the winter and summer.

What about the clothes you buy at the store? With no electricity, there'd be no factories to make clothes to sell. You'd probably only have one or two handmade outfits that you'd have to wear every day for years and years, sewing them up every time they ripped.

While you're at it, throw out your TV, video games, music CDs, and cell phones. They'd be useless anyway because you're not going to have anything to power them with. Although, they might make good paper weights.

Yet, as shocking as all this sounds, people lived without electricity for thousands of years. It was only within the last century that electricity became widely used. Some of you might even have relatives who once lived in houses without electricity.

Without electricity, a lot of your favorite things wouldn't work. They probably never would have even been invented!

Chapter 2

I Have It All Under Control

To: ProfMaxPower

From: AmandaSanchez99

Professor Power, now that we know what electricity is made of, is there any way to control it?

There are three things we need to control electricity: a **conductor**, a **circuit**, and an **insulator**. A conductor is something for the electricity to travel through. Most metals make great conductors. We use long, thin metal conductors in the shape of wires to control the flow of electric energy, the direction it travels in, and the amount of electricity we want to use.

Electricity loves to make a connection. If you have a power source (like an electric outlet) and a conductor (like a metal wire), then both ends of the conductor wire must be connected to the power source. This creates a circuit, which is a circular path for the electricity to travel around and around on.

A connection is made.

Oops, the connection's broken. Lights out!

As long as the circuit is unbroken, you have a flow of electricity. But if the conductor wire is cut or breaks, then so is the connection—and you're left in the dark.

The last thing we need to control electricity is an insulator. Insulators are for safety. You'll notice that the electric cords to the appliances in your home are covered in plastic. That plastic is the cord's insulator.

Inside the plastic insulator is a wire—that's right, the conductor wire. It goes from the electric outlet in the wall to the appliance and then back out again to the wall, completing the circuit.

But you can't go around grabbing conductor wires with electricity running through them! That's where the insulator comes in. Electricity cannot pass through plastic or rubber, so electric cords are covered in plastic so that you can handle them safely.

Flow of Electricity Through a Circuit

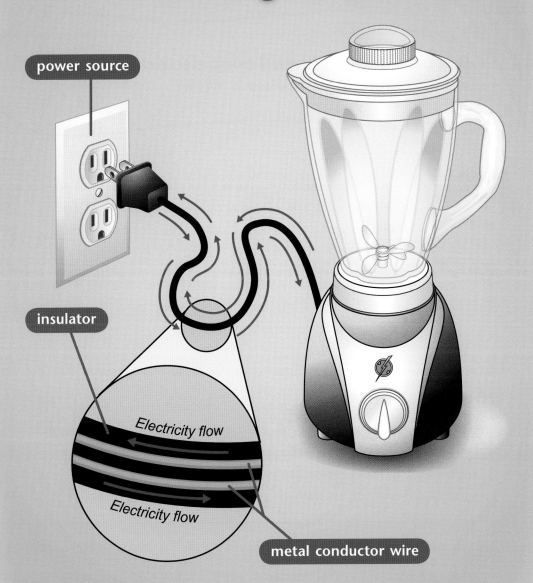

power source

insulator

Electricity flow

Electricity flow

metal conductor wire

To: ProfMaxPower

From: JillHill

Professor Power, I know I need electricity to power a light bulb, but how does it work?

Excellent question, Miss Hill. The light bulb seems simple, yet it took Thomas Edison hundreds of tries before he got it to work. In fact, the design of the bulb in the lamps of today hasn't changed much since Edison's time. They are both made of four things:

- conductor wires for electricity to travel through,
- a metal wire called a **filament**,
- a gas called argon,
- and a glass bulb to put it all in.

Here's how it works. An electric **current** runs through the conductor wires into the filament, which is a special kind of metal that can be heated for long periods of time without melting. Filament wires are extremely thin. They are one-hundredth of an inch thick and coiled very tightly.

The electricity heats the filament to very high temperatures where it will glow brightly and give off light. The argon is there to make sure the filament doesn't catch fire. Unlike oxygen, argon is a gas that does not combust, meaning it won't burn.

Put all these parts together in a glass bulb, add some electricity, and you've seen the light!

argon

glass bulb

filament

conductor wires

Thomas Edison was one of America's greatest inventors. In addition to the light bulb, Edison also invented the world's first phonograph and movie camera.

The first light bulbs would only burn for about 13 hours. Today there are bulbs that last for 20,000 hours.

To: ProfMaxPower

From: MacavityCat

I know we can control the electricity in our house, but what about other electricity, like lightning?

Mac is right on track! When a storm cloud is full of rain, it has a bunch of negatively charged electrons at the bottom and positively charged electrons at the top. If ice is present in the cloud, it helps increase the strength of the two charges. If a cloud has all of these things, it forms a powerful **electric field**.

Lightning flashes occur when the electric fields of two clouds trade electrons and charges of electricity. The lightning we see is the path of electrons moving from one cloud to another. These electrons follow a very narrow path, which is why lightning appears in narrow, jagged bolts.

Lightning strikes the ground when charged electrons in a cloud's electric field connect with charged electrons on the earth. You get a bolt of electricity passing between the two that is hotter than the surface of the sun!

In other words, there's no way for science, at the moment, to control such a powerful force of nature.

But you can't have lightning without thunder, right? Right. Thunder is caused by air that has been super-heated by lightning. We've already said that lightning is very hot (about 18,000° Fahrenheit), but it also travels very fast. It therefore heats the air around it very quickly. When the air heats up, the air molecules inside of it spread out. This expansion happens so fast and with such force that the air pretty much explodes. We hear this explosion as thunder booming through the sky.

The reason you hear thunder *after* you see lightning is because of the different speeds at which light and sound travel. Light travels much faster than sound, so even though the two happen at the same time, you'll see the lightning first. Seconds later, depending on how far away the storm is, you'll hear the thunder.

Throughout history, different cultures around the world have tried to explain the cause of thunder and lightning. Some cultures believed that thunder came from the gods. The Norse god of thunder was Thor, who had a huge hammer that rocked the heavens when he swung it.

Chapter 3

Charge It Up!

To: ProfMaxPower

From: MrCGeorge

There's electricity in socks, lamps, and lightning... but can we *make* electricity?

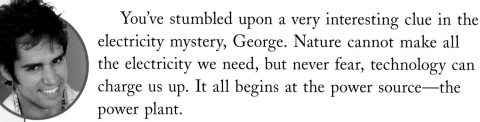

You've stumbled upon a very interesting clue in the electricity mystery, George. Nature cannot make all the electricity we need, but never fear, technology can charge us up. It all begins at the power source—the power plant.

The first ingredient in making electricity is heat. The power plant gets its heat by burning fossil fuels. The heat boils water inside huge boiler tanks, and that creates a lot of steam which hits a giant wheel called a turbine. The turbine has blades like a fan, and the steam blows through these blades, making them spin.

The spinning turbine turns a rod attached to a **generator**. The generator charges electrons that jump around and make, you guessed it—electricity.

After the power plant, electricity flows through power lines to a power station, where it's stored until needed. All this raw electricity has to pass through a transformer before going to your house.

A transformer is a metal drum attached to a telephone pole that sends electricity to a house or building. We measure electricity by **volts**. Electricity from a power station can be more than 20,000 volts, which is more than a single house can safely handle. The transformer only lets a safe amount of electricity through to your house—only about 220 volts, which is plenty. Anything more could do some serious damage!

Power lines are an important part of getting power to your house. The lines carry the electricity, and transformer drums safely control how much power is sent to a house.

Getting Power to Your Home

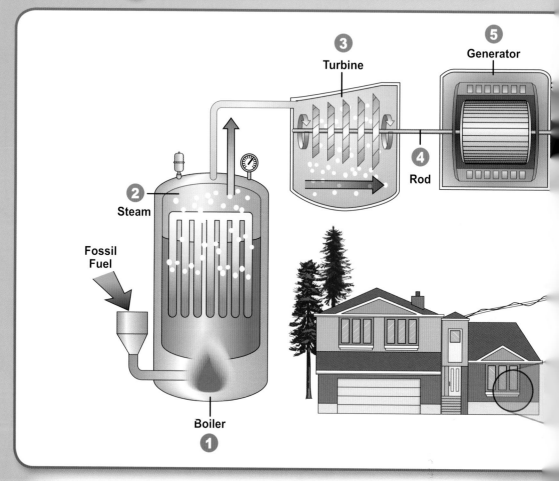

1. Fuel is burned in a boiler to create heat.
2. The heat causes water to boil, making steam.
3. The steam turns the turbine.
4. The turbine turns the rod that goes into the generator.

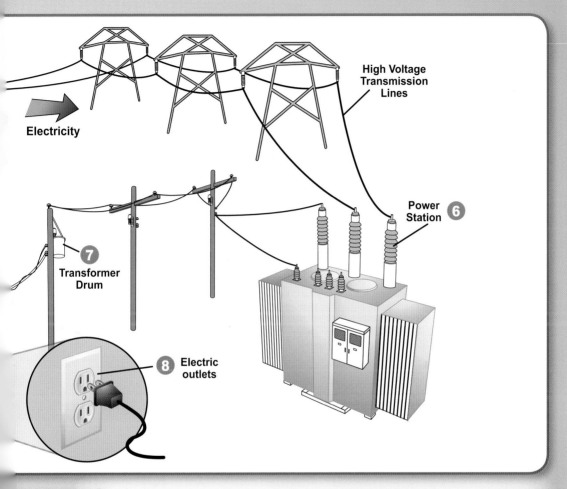

High Voltage
Transmission
Lines

Electricity

Power
Station **6**

7
Transformer
Drum

8 Electric
outlets

5 The generator charges electrons that make electricity.

6 The electricity travels through high voltage transmission lines to a power station.

7 From there, electricity goes to transformer drums, which send it through wires to individual buildings and homes.

8 People plug appliances into electric outlets to use the electricity.

Oil, coal, and natural gas are fossil fuels. They take millions of years to form. Once we've burned them, they're gone. They cannot be used over and over again. Many people fear we will one day use up all the earth's fossil fuels.

The steam that is used to turn the turbines can reach temperatures of 1,000°F. These factory workers watch the equipment to make sure everything runs smoothly.

To: ProfMaxPower

From: BusyBee

Are there other ways of making electricity, Professor Power?

There are other ways, Bee. Take out your calculator. Chances are, it uses solar power to do its math.

Remember me saying that power plants burn fossil fuels? The important thing to know about solar power, wind power, and water power is that they don't need fossil fuels to make electricity.

solar calculator

Solar means "from the sun," so solar power is power we get from the sun. Solar powered calculators, road signs, cars, and even houses all have shiny, silver plates, called solar panels, to catch the sun's rays. Solar panels absorb sunlight. Once inside the panels, the sunlight stirs up electrons. This gives the electrons a charge, and as we've seen, charged electrons are what electrical energy is all about.

Unfortunately, solar power does not provide enough electricity for us to get rid of power plants altogether. However, scientists are working to make solar power more powerful and useful.

Solar power can run this house and fuel up this race car, but right now it can't supply enough power to run everyone's house and everyone's car. There's just too many of them.

We can also get power from the wind—just think *windmills*.

Windmills have been around since the 7th century B.C., but the windmills of today are much more high-tech. Instead of using steam to turn the turbines in a power plant, wind power turns the turbine blades of a windmill. All you need is a really windy place.

Wind farms are areas with hundreds of wind-powered turbines towering high above the ground. The largest wind farm in the United States is in Alamont Pass, California. It has more than 6,000 wind turbines generating electricity.

Or instead of using wind, you could use water! Water mills have also been around for thousands of years. They are built on the side of a river and have a large wheel stuck right into the water that acts as the turbine. As the river flows by, it turns the wheel.

Hook up a generator to this water wheel, and you've got a small power plant going. The faster the river flows, the faster the wheel turns, and the more electricity you can produce.

The amount of thick, grey smog is different for different cities. Seattle, Washington, has less smog than Los Angeles, California. Can you tell which is which?

New discoveries in solar, wind, and water power are important. The fossil fuels burned in power plants cannot be reused, meaning they can all be burned up. Once they're gone, so is our ability to make electricity. But we'll never run out of sun, water, or wind. These things are renewable, so we can always have more.

Also, the burning of fossil fuels is harmful to the environment. The smoke they produce releases pollutants like carbon monoxide and sulfur dioxide. These gases rise into the air and mix with fog to make a thick, dark cloud called smog. Smog hangs over areas where lots of fossil fuels are burned, and it can make it harder for people to breathe.

Chapter 4

Electricity and Magnetism

To: | ProfMaxPower

From: | ChicagoMike

Max, I've heard people talk about electromagnets. Is that some sort of cross between electricity and magnets?

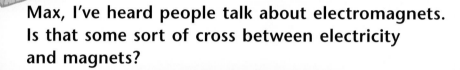

You've got it, Mike. The *electro-* part, as you may have guessed, means "having to do with electricity." So, electromagnets are magnets made from electricity.

Magnetism is the force that attracts or **repels** metal objects. Magnets have positive charges and negative charges, just like the particles that make electricity. Opposite charges, such as positive/negative, attract each other. Similar charges, such as positive/positive or negative/negative, repel each other.

Now then, you can make a magnet out of an ordinary metal object by putting an electric charge through it. The particles in the atoms still have their positive and negative charges—and now, so does the metal object!

Juice it up with enough electricity, and the object will have a very strong magnetic pull. Take the electricity away, and the object goes back to being an ordinary metal object.

Electric Energy

Important Characteristics:
- Positive and negative charges
- Opposites attract
- Made of charged electrons

Things that conduct electricity:
- Metals
- Acids
- Water

Insulators of electricity:
- Plastic • Rubber
- Glass • Wood

Magnetic Energy

Important Characteristics:
- Positive and negative charges
- Opposites attract
- Made of charged electrons

Things that magnets attract:
- Metals

Things magnets do not attract:
- Plastic • Rubber
- Glass • Wood

As you can see, electricity and magnetism have a lot of things in common. The first person to discover the relationship between the two was an English scientist named Michael Faraday.

In 1831, Faraday noticed that if he placed a metal wire near a magnet, an electric current, or a flow of charged electrons, passed through the wire. The current wasn't very strong, but he soon learned that he could make it stronger by using a stronger magnet. Not only that, but the more wire he wrapped around the magnet, the stronger the electric current became.

The magnetic levitation train uses electromagnetism instead of wheels. The train floats along the track and travels at 150 miles per hour.

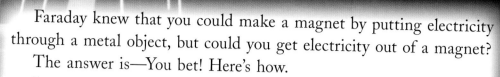

Faraday knew that you could make a magnet by putting electricity through a metal object, but could you get electricity out of a magnet?

The answer is—You bet! Here's how.

In a magnet, opposites attract. Negative charges in one magnet pull positive charges in another magnet toward it. If you keep the two magnets close together, electrons will jump from one to the other. And what happens when electrons get to jumping? You get electricity! If the magnets aren't very strong, then the electric charge will be very weak, but it's still there.

This is what electromagnetism is all about. The magnet Faraday wrapped in wire was one of the first electromagnets. Today we have electromagnets that are strong enough to lift a car.

Michael Faraday was a great British inventor. He once said, "Nothing is too wonderful to be true."

Hi, Pumpkin! You mentioned that a magnet has poles. Is that anything like the earth's north pole and south pole?

Aunt Martha? Ugh, please don't call me that name! :)

To answer your question, it's exactly like the earth's north pole and south pole. In fact, imagine the earth as having a huge bar magnet running through the middle of it. The earth, like the bar magnet, has two poles which are areas of strongest magnetic charge.

This imaginary bar magnet creates the huge magnetic field surrounding the earth. Yet, it does not run perfectly up and down. It's tilted slightly. The "geographic north" pole sits at the exact top of the globe, while the "magnetic north" pole is 11.3° to the side.

The earth's magnetic field is too weak to feel, but there's an easy way to know it's there.

Hikers often use a simple device called a compass. A compass is nothing more than a magnetized metal needle resting on a point so it can turn freely. The needle's magnetic current is attracted to magnetic north, and so, the needle will always point north. If you're ever lost in the woods, pull out your compass. It may not direct you to a phone, but at least you will know which direction you're going.

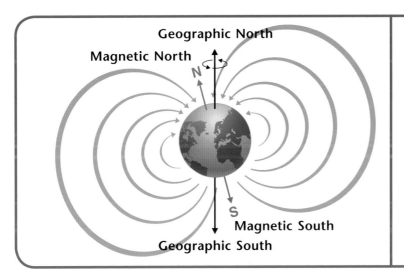

Geographic North
Magnetic North

N

S

Magnetic South
Geographic South

These arrows show the magnetic field surrounding the earth. The magnetic poles are at the top and bottom of the globe.

No matter where you are on the earth, the compass's needle will always point north.

Chapter 5

Portable Power

To: ProfMaxPower

From: EddyGorey

I hate being tied down, Max. Do we always have to be "plugged in" to get electricity?

What's up, Eddy? You want something that's easy to carry around with you, right? Luckily, there's an easy way to produce electricity that you can take with you. These things run some of the games and devices you have at home, like a flashlight. I'm talking about batteries! Batteries are like mini-power plants that fit in your hand. They work without fuel, heat, boiling water, steam, turbines, generators, or electromagnets. Instead, batteries generate electricity using certain metals and chemicals to conduct electricity.

In 1800, an Italian **physicist** named Alessandro Volta discovered a new way to produce a steady electric current. He stacked a disk of copper with a positive charge on top of a disk of zinc with a negative charge. Then, he separated the two with paper soaked in salt water to help increase the conductivity, which is the ability to transport electricity.

The charged electrons in the copper and zinc began jumping from positive to negative across the paper, and you know what that means—electricity! Not only that, but the electric currents kept going and going. Volta discovered that the higher the stack, the more powerful the electricity it made.

Volta's invention was called the "artificial electrical organ," or more simply, "Volta's pile."

Other scientists began experimenting with Volta's ideas. They used liquid chemicals between the copper and zinc instead of salty paper. This worked better, but still, who'd want to carry around a bunch of chemicals in their MP3 player?

In the twentieth century, scientists developed a way to use chemicals in a dry form so they were much easier to carry around. The chemicals were mixed with a paste that kept the positive charge on one side of the battery and the negative charge on the other. Over time, these batteries became smaller and more powerful, until you have the battery of today.

Does the name *Volta* sound familiar? From Volta's name we get the words *volt* and *voltage*.

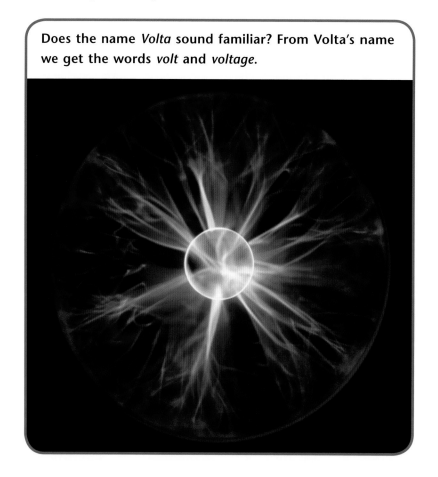

Volta's Pile and the Modern Battery

Open up a flashlight. You'll notice the metal tabs labeled "positive" (+) and "negative" (-). When batteries are placed inside the flashlight, these metal tabs direct the electric current from the battery into the flashlight.

Volta's Pile

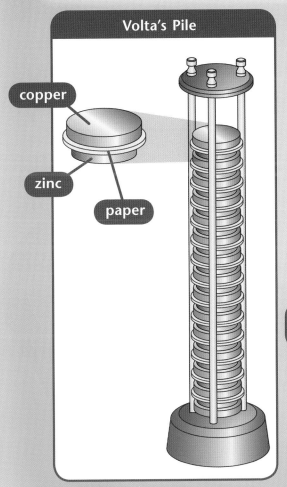

copper

zinc

paper

Modern Battery

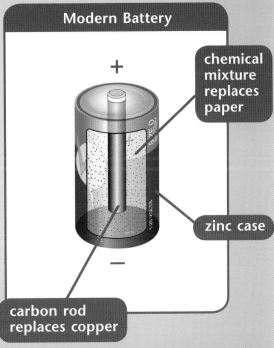

+

chemical mixture replaces paper

zinc case

carbon rod replaces copper

Volta's pile was the first of its kind, but it can't compare with the power and ease of today's batteries.

The Electricity Mystery

Over the last several chapters, I've answered a lot of e-mails, and you've seen a lot of new and exciting things about electric energy. But what exactly is the electricity mystery?

Here's a little science experiment that should help shine a light on things. We'll be making electricity using a homemade battery, so get ready to use everything we've learned so far.

Be sure to grab an adult to be your lab assistant for this experiment. They might learn something!

Now then, the dime and penny are your metals, the lemon provides the chemical, the wire is your conductor, and the bulb is your appliance.

You'll need:
- lemon
- small knife
- penny
- dime
- small flashlight bulb
- copper wire

When you've got everything together, follow these steps to produce an electric current:

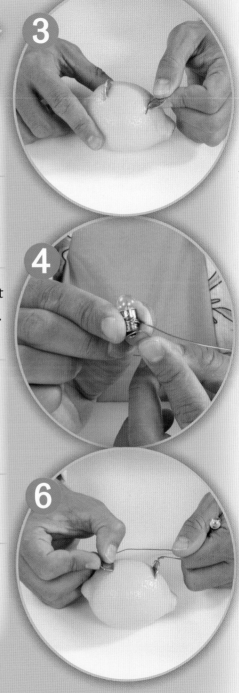

❶ Press and roll the lemon on a flat surface to get the lemon juices flowing.

❷ Ask your lab assistant to use the knife to cut two slits in the lemon.

❸ Place the penny halfway into one slit and the dime halfway into the other. The two coins must not touch.

❹ Wrap the copper wire around the bottom of the flashlight bulb several times. Be sure to leave some wire dangling at the ends.

❺ Wrap one end of the wire around the penny, which is your copper.

❻ Wrap the other end of the wire around the dime, which is your zinc.

Check out the bulb. You should be able to see it lighting up at least a little. The lemon battery won't be enough to power it all the way, but you'll see that you've made an electric current using fruit!

How can a lemon make electricity? The penny, the dime, and the lemon juice create an electric current, just like Volta's pile. The charged electrons jump from the copper to the zinc. This current flows through the circuit of wires and into the bulb. It then heats up the bulb's filament, and you have light!

Now that we've seen electricity in action, what does it all mean? What's the answer to the electricity mystery?

The mystery is that there is no mystery! Electricity might seem mysterious, but we've seen how the charged electrons in an atom produce an electric current and how that current is used to power things in your home, like a light bulb. We've seen ways in which electricity can be generated, where lightning comes from, what role magnets play in electric energy, and how batteries make power more portable.

Thanks for all the wonderful e-mails you guys sent me. Hopefully, understanding electricity is now a breeze. The only mystery left is what's next for Max Power?

Glossary

appliance a machine or device you use in your house, like a refrigerator or television

atom the smallest piece matter can be broken up into

circuit a circular path that electricity travels on

conductor a piece of metal that carries electricity very easily

current a flow of electricity

electric field an area with a strong electric charge

filament a very thin metal wire that's used as a conductor

generator a machine that turns motion into electricity

insulator something that blocks electricity

matter the material that makes up physical objects

molecule a group of atoms that is used to make matter

particle a small part of something

physicist a scientist that studies atoms and matter

repel to push away

static not moving or changing

volt the unit of measurement used to measure electricity

Index